To David Roschoug in memory of Brie

God is

THE HAND OF GOD

Vahan Hovey

A True Testimony of God's Love and Faithfulness

By

VAHAN HOVEY

xulon PRESS

FOREWORD

The accounts of place, things and people in this book are entirely true. After sixty some odd years of incubating in my memory, I have decided to share my testimony of what God can do. Believing in him as the Creator and Master of all things can give one the strength and courage to face any and all the tribulations and trials that life on this Earth can and will impose on mere mortals. It is my fondest wish and hope that perhaps even one soul will find the comfort and strength needed by turning to Him as the Lord of your life after reading this book.

As a matter of clarification, I would like to point out that when I entered the service, I was Vahan Hovhannissian, an Armenian immigrant who came to this country at the age of three. After graduation from college, I entered show business and changed my name, for obvious reasons, to Vahan Hovey. From that I embarked on various other careers all of which were successful in their own way. I can honestly say that "walking the good walk and talking the good talk" have been a driving force in helping me to "live the good life". I recommend it to all.

TABLE OF CONTENTS

PART ONE

PART TWO

Chapter 1

THE UNEXPECTED

B ullets have their own peculiar way of announcing their arrival in your vicinity. That distinctive cracking sound as a bullet breaks the sound barrier is all the warning you will get when you're in someone's sights. So it was on that cold January morning in 1945 as we were plodding through fresh falling snow on an offensive thrust assigned to "clear out a pocket of German soldiers" in a patch of woods known as the Hagenau forest just outside the town of Gamshein, Germany. We were told it would be a "piece of cake" since Intelligence determined that only ninety or so

Germans were in that forest and we went after them with an entire battalion!

Crack! Crack! Crack! Crack!

Bullets were whistling close to my head! Instinct and training told me, without a second thought, hit the dirt!

Where are they? I couldn't see anything but a pristine row of trees covered with nature's regal mantle of lily white snow. I raised my head higher for a better look when the soldier nearest to me screamed a fearsome gasp…then fell silent.

For him the war was over.

Our platoon leader shouted out, "pull back, pull back".

With the multiple layers of clothing I was wearing topped by a bulky, white camouflage suit, turning around in eight inches of snow while keeping a low profile was not the easiest maneuver to negotiate. Meanwhile, bullets were flying, mortar shells were dropping, cannons were booming and, as if orchestrated like Tchaikovsky's 1812 Overture, men were moaning and screaming as steel ripped through flesh and bone. It was the most intense barrage of enemy fire I had ever personally witnessed thus far in the war.

Then it happened.

Like a branding iron charged with 10,000 volts of electricity, the bullet I never heard tore into my left leg, passed through it and then into the other leg. Every muscle in my body tensed, every nerve seemed to relay the pain and the shock to my brain. I've been shot! In that split second, a veritable endless stream of thoughts raced through my mind like a cassette tape on fast forward.

Does this me that I am that I am going to die?

If I survive, will I lose my legs and end up in a wheelchair the rest of my life? I couldn't bear the thought of people looking at me and feeling sorry.

Does this mean that I'll never dance again? Oh, how I loved to dance and was darn good at it too.

How will my family react when they get the dreaded telegram? I couldn't bear that image at all.

Will I be buried right here or will they send my body back home?

What will happen to all the war mementos I've collected? The Lugar, the Bayonet, the German Medal, the camera, all stashed in my duffel bag.

Now that someone has me in their sights, will I be shot again for good measure?

What do I do? What do I do?

I've never been shot before!

I can't reach for my first aid kit.

I can't call for a medic.

I can't do anything but maybe die!

But wait; there is something I can do! The most important thing I can do, I can pray! I hadn't got much further than "Dear God, is this to be the end?" when my attention was suddenly focused on a new, unexpected peril. Evidently, I had crawled into the line of fire of a machine gun because now I could feel a tugging and pulling on my camouflage suit as the constant sound of bullets increased.

Crack! Crack! Crack! Crack! In rapid succession.

Oh my God, I thought, the bullets are ripping right through my clothes! How long will it be before the Gunner drops his sights a half inch and cuts me in half with his bullets!

I hugged the ground.

I hugged the snow.

I exhaled all I could –and – I prayed as never before!

"Dear Lord, please don't let me die like this. You know I promised my mother that I would surely return from the war – not to worry. How could I go back on my word especially after my mother had assured me that "God will watch over you". It just wouldn't be fair for her to lose her faith after having gone through so much suffering in her life with an unswerving faith and trust in your bountiful mercy".

My prayers were swiftly answered.

It was as if a giant hand came down and pushed me further into the ground. I felt formlessly thin – flesh and boneless – just flat. Bullets kept ripping my clothes without finding their intended target and I kept praying for deliverance, suddenly at peace, and without any further fear as the blissful oblivion of unconsciousness transported me to another place.

The noise, the pain, the fear, the anxiety all passed away as my thoughts drifted back to the train station in my hometown of Mount Vernon, New York. My mother, father, grandmother, sister, kid brother were there plus my high school sweetheart Virginia and my best friend George. Everyone, except my older brother who had gone into the service just three months before me. It was February, 1943, and I had just turned eighteen and graduated from high school. Full of patriotic fervor, I volunteered rather than waiting for the draft. Grandmother Victoria reminded me of her faith had sustained her as she fled from the Turkish Massacre of Armenians in 1919 with her three daughters (one was my mother) and my mother's toddler son (my brother in the service). The Turks had already killed my grandfather and my mother's husband as it was their policy since 1915 to kill all Armenian males of any age. For this reason, my mother had dressed my brother as a girl and safely passed through many searches during their exodus from the country. With a band of Turkish regulars dogging this little band of women, bent on committing the many atrocities that the Devil would have them bringing down on Christian Armenian women, the Hand of God led them to the gates of a Presbyterian Missionary near the border with Iran. Here they were sheltered and fed and eventually escorted to safety in Iran.

For some inexplicable reason, the Turkish soldiers honored the sanctuary of this Mission and did nor pursue any further. As a matter of fact, they even begged for and received food before going on their way.

Seeking solace and safety with other Christians was not strange for Armenians because of their long history of Christian faith. After all, it was the Armenians who became the very first nation in the world to accept Christ as their savior and declared Christianity as the National Religion in the year 301 A.D. It was in gratitude for this missionary kindness and sanctuary that my mother instructed her children to attend the Presbyterian Church after our family had migrated to America even though we officially belonged to the Armenian Apostolic Church. After fleeing to Iran, my mother married again and had three children – my sister, kid brother and me (not counting a brother who died in infancy). My sister and I walked to church every Sunday (a distance of one and one-half miles). From the age of nine to twelve, I was chosen soloist for our senior choir. After my beautiful soprano voice changed, I continued in the choir, but also began teaching Sunday School to the little children. God had been a very pivotal part of my life to this point and there was no reason to think that He would not continue to "watch over me" as my mother assured me that day on the platform.

The most consistent strain running through my childhood was the Lord's Prayer and the 23rd Psalm. "The Lord is my shepherd" – literally described the salvation of my family before and after I was born. We recited these prayers almost every night and especially, the 23rd Psalm during those dark days of the Great Depression when my family had scant resources and barely enough to eat.

And now it took on a new meaning for me as I literally found myself "walking through the valley of the shadow of death".

Chapter 2

RIGHT IN DER FUHRER'S FACE

It was November, 1944, when our outfit, the 12th Armored Division, was ordered up to the front lines to relieve units of the 45th Infantry. The driving rain and unforgiving cold wind of southern France was more punishing than the thought of enemy fire. After three days and nights of riding in open flat bed trucks and then on top of our own tanks, all in a steady bone-chilling downpour, we were deployed into fox holes being vacated by those tired dogfaces. During our first night in a two-man foxhole, I was suddenly gripped by chills, fever and the unmistakable cramps of oncoming diarrhea. I couldn't hold it any longer. I told my foxhole buddy that I gotta go NOW – no matter what!

"But where?" he asked "there is nothing but open fields around us and deep tank tracks in the ankle deep mud.

"That's it!" I said. "The tank tracks about 50 yards away would make a perfect slit trench!"

"But those *Screeming Meemees* raining down on us along with nature's soaking – what about them?"

I replied, "I don't give a damn?" I scurried out of the foxhole and over to the 'slit trench'. As I was pulling down my pants, a funny thought entered my mind. The strains of a very popular song of the times by Spike Jones and the City Slickers – "Right In The Fuhrer's Face!" echoed over and over again. That's it! I thought as I turned my back to the enemy and squatted over the tank rut. I sang it out loud, "Frrt, Frrt, Right in the Fuhrer's Face!"

Those awesome 88mm shells were dropping all around me, my buddies were calling me back but I didn't care. I found ultimate relief and patted myself on the back for making such a profound statement thanks to Spike Jones.

I dragged myself back to the foxhole amid cheers and jeers only to find that urge come upon me fifteen minutes later. My buddy said, "Not again, you gotta be nuts!"

"Would you rather I did it here in the foxhole?, I replied.

Not having considered the unpleasantry, he said, "be careful"

I told him that "I trust in the Hand of God to watch over me so I have no fear".

Then the same scenario unfolded. Me over the tank rut, my back to the enemy, and those satisfying strains of Spike Jones' ditty "Frtt, Frtt, Right in the Fuhrer's Face!" while those *Screaming Meemees* dropped on all sides.

Dragging myself back to the foxhole was a real test of determination and endurance in my weakened condition. Someone called for a medic who crawled up to my position a short while later and stuffed a thermometer in my mouth. "104 ½" he whistled "I better go tell the Captain".

He returned a short while later with permission to escort me back to our Aid Station. By the time we got to the Aid

Tent another thermometer in my mouth and another reading 105!

"This soldier has to be rushed to the Hospital. There's a good chance we have pneumonia here" said the field doctor at the Aid Station. Arriving at the Hospital by ambulance 30 minutes later, my temperature had climbed to 106!

By this time I was quite delirious with a burning in my head that felt like my brain was being fried. Nothing more was done, but Quinine pills by the handful several times a day. The fever finally broke about the third day.

"About two weeks of recuperation and you should be able to rejoin your outfit", I was told by my attending doctor.

Could the "hand of God" put me here in this Hospital for another reason? I wondered.

The second day that I was up and around walking about the Hospital turned out to be December 24, 1944.

"Tonight is Christmas Eve" I thought. There ought to be a service I must attend. I asked everyone who might know and found that there was no service scheduled and no Chaplain available to perform one. I asked if there was a piano in the hospital and the answer was negative. Finally, one of the orderlies I had questioned said that he thought that there was a small field organ stuck in one of the closets. We hurried to the spot and dragged out this little field organ which was all folded up like a large suitcase. It was about three feet long and three feet tall fully opened with foot pedals that had to be pumped while playing in order to blow air into the reeds thereby making organ music. It seemed like a primitive relic but a little experimentation showed that it really worked?

I had never in my life played an organ let alone this contraption that had to be pumped as you played it. I gave it a shot though and found that it wasn't all that difficult after you got the hang of it.

I had no music, nor had I ever played Christmas music before, but I had sung all the carols and still remembered most of the words.

"Tonight there will be a Christmas Eve Service" I told the orderly. "Pass the word around to anyone interested that we will meet in the lounge tonight at 10 o'clock.

They came from everywhere. Patients hobbling in, those on crutches, some in wheelchairs, doctors, men in uniform, men in pajamas, everyone who heard about the service. The room overflowed with bodies – into the hallways, on the stairs, on the floor. I was first overwhelmed with happiness then seized with an overwhelming panic!

What if I can't play this organ? What if I don't remember the carols? What if I make mistakes and they all laugh at me?"

"Dear Lord, please guide my hands to play, please let me remember the words and to say the right things and bring glory to this holy of all holy nights." I shuffled out in front of the crowd in my hospital-issued bathrobe and slippers. Clearing my throat, I said "Let's begin our celebration of Christmas with Joy to the World".

My fingers found their way and my voice rang out the words – and they followed! "Let's do it again" came a voice from the rear. So we sang it again and again, each time a little louder and, each time, a little fuller as more voices chimed in. Several more carols followed. "O Little Town of

Bethlehem", "Hark the Herald Angels Sing", "O Come All Ye Faithful".

It didn't matter what a person's religion. They all sang, they all came on crutches, wheelchairs, bandaged, walking – whatever – they that could come came.

Then, there was an awkward silence as the mood reflected homesick thoughts of loved ones and Christmases past. There was no Chaplain so I stood up from my organ and found words I had never uttered before.

"We come together tonight not to only sing carols but to commemorate the birth of Jesus Christ almost 2,000 years ago. Yes, Jesus is the reason for this season and we are gathered here to praise that glorious birth that was a fulfillment of prophesies foretold centuries earlier. Whether you believe he was the Messiah or not, there is no mistaking the love that He taught and the feeling of love and peace that we all feel here tonight. Let us pray that this war will be over soon and that we will be celebrating next Christmas back home with our families and dear ones in total peace and harmony".

Then as we were singing "Silent Night" a spontaneous thing happened. Someone turned most of the lights off and from somewhere (probably the nurses) a few candles appeared around the room. And in that glimmering light one could see wet eyes in every direction and streamlets flowing down many cheeks while sniffles and breaking voices pierced that blanket of somberness and serenity that ended with "sleep in heavenly peace".

I lost it then. I just sat at the organ for a while as the bodies quietly filed back to their wards. It was then that a major in full uniform approached me and asked "Soldier, are you in Special Services?" (that branch of Army designated to entertain troops).

"No" I replied, "just a dogface in the 12th Armored Division".

He took my name, serial number and outfit and promised to contact a friend of his at headquarters who might manage a transfer for me to Special Services. "We could certainly use someone like you doing exactly what you did tonight". And with that last statement he departed, and unfortunately,

I recovered sufficiently to be sent back to my outfit before any such orders came through. I was only back with my old outfit four days when, on January 15, 1945, we were ordered on the offensive to clear out some German soldiers in the Hagenau Forest.

Chapter 3

LUCKY STRIKES

Mercifully, I must have passed out from loss of blood for the next thing I remember was being back on the battlefield and becoming startled by the sharp report of a rifle being fired very close to my ear. I slowly opened my eyes to see one of my buddies with his rifle resting on my back as he fired away at the enemy.

"What the hell are you doing?" I snapped.

"Oh, I thought you were dead – sorry" and with that he scrambled over to another body as if it were a log and started blindly firing away at the enemy again.

That soldier's name was Orville Hollerman, a squirrel-hunting farm boy from Kentucky. Orville and I had the distinction of being he best marksmen in our company on the rifle range. Now, here he was using me for a shield like some decaying log in the forest and still "squirrel-hunting".

That was the last time I saw him.

"Oh God, thank you for keeping the squirrels from shooting back at Orville. And, if they did, thank you for making them shoot too high". With this prayer on my lips, I drifted in and out of consciousness until sometime in the afternoon. It was then that I became aware of a deafening silence!

No more shooting! No more screaming! No more cannons! – Nothing!

I turned my head to the other side just in time to see someone waving a white piece of cloth stuck on the end of a bayoneted rifle about two hundred feet away. Our boys are surrendering – what now!

Wait a minute! We're not supposed to lose the battle. They were supposed to be 90 or so men and we had a whole battalion of over 800 including 20 tanks!

As I learned much later, the Germans had set a well-designed trap for us and executed it beautifully!

First, they situated their position on the reverse slope of a long hill. This put them at the bottom where they had a perfect view of everyone and everything that came over the top of the hill heading down towards their position.

Second, they allowed our forward units to capture their sentries to lull us into thinking we were surprising them.

Thirdly, it was not a band of 90 Germans as they wanted our intelligence to think It was, in reality, what was left of an entire crack Panzer Division with all their tanks and personnel! Even at reduced strength, this meant over 5,000 soldiers and over 25 Tiger tanks!

The final outcome of this debacle was 80% casualties among our men, all 20 of our tanks destroyed or disabled and the walking wounded and other survivors taken prisoner.

There were virtually no survivors to carry on the Battalion as a working unit. For all intents and purposes, the 66th Armored Infantry Battalion was wiped out!

A short time later I opened my eyes to see a group of German soldiers walking up the battlefield carrying pistols! Then it dawned on me. Just a few days ago I had read in our paper "The Stars And Stripes" that, since the Battle of the Bulge, Germans were not taking any wounded prisoners! Their facilities were overburdened with their own and the logistics of caring for wounded prisoners were too much of a burden in this stage of the war. So, the solution was that all wounded enemy soldiers not able to walk were SHOT DEAD!

Not too much time to think. What am I going to do? They're coming closer. Bang! Oh God, they're doing it! Bang! Bang! Two more! More Bangs!

I can hear their footsteps now!

Then the plan. I'll play dead! I'll wait until dark and then I'll crawl back to my lines, tell them all what happened and maybe become a hero by doing it.

I was lying prone on my stomach when I felt searching hands going through my pockets. Then my watch was taken and someone tried to take my high school ring but it wouldn't come off. Fortunately it looked cheap enough to be forgotten. Then I felt hands grab my arm to turn me over.

"Dear God, don't let me make a sound from the pain. Don't let me open my eyes!"

Over I went as I held my breath and tried to be as limp as possible. The pain shot through both legs as they searched my pockets. Of course, my camouflage suit (which was like a bed sheet with a hole cut out for one's head) was covering everything. I could feel my eyes want to open. I just couldn't control it any longer. They would see my eyes open and then I would see the cold barrel thrust against my temple. But then a hand – someone's hand—picked up the bottom of my camouflage suit and threw it over my face! Now they could get at my overcoat pockets and look for whatever. My eyes opened to see this sea of white covered with huge blotches of bright red. As I silently gave thanks for not being discovered,

I felt myself drifting off as the muttering soldiers moved away to find better pickings.

The next thing I remember was darkness.

"Ah, here's my chance" I thought. Now all is quiet and I'll just crawl back to my lines and this ordeal can finally come to an end. (Never mind that it was at least a mile or more back to our point of demarcation.)

First, I had to roll over on my stomach. That didn't take too long but now I had to crawl. I dug my elbows into the snow beside my body and gave a push. Nothing! Both legs were completely limp – like they didn't even exist.

Try again. Nothing!

I've got to move more than two inches – this is ridiculous!

Try again. Nothing!

No more strength or energy in my arms, elbows or body. That's it! I'm not going to make it. I'm too weak from loss of blood. They will probably find my body stiff as a board tomorrow sometime. I'll never last the night in this cold. I can't feel my feet or my hands anymore. There is nothing else to do.

But wait, what did my grandmother say they did in the face of the Turks?

"Our father who art in heaven hallowed be they name
They kingdom come, thy will be done
On earth as it is in heaven.
Give us this day our daily bread and forgive us our
trespasses
As we forgive those that trespass against us
And lead us not into temptation, but deliver us from evil
For thine is the kingdom, and the power, and the glory
for ever and ever. Amen"

And there's more! The 23rd Psalm.

"The Lord is my shepherd, I shall not want
He makes me lie down in green pastures
He leads me by the still waters, He restores my Soul.

He leads me in the paths of righteousness for his names
sake

Ye, though I walk through the valley of the shadow of
death

I will fear no evil

For thou art with me

Thy rod and thy staff they comfort me

You prepare a table before me

Even in the face of my enemies

You anoint my head with oil

My cup runneth over

Surely Goodness and Mercy will be with me all the days
of my life

And I will dwell in the House of the Lord Forever!
Amen.

That's the one! Say it again and then say it again.

Preparing to die is not easy, but the thought of going to
Heaven to be with Jesus and the Angels brought me such

peace that I found myself looking forward to this new and final experience.

My prayers and reveries were suddenly interrupted by the sound of footsteps crunching snow as they moved ever closer to where I lay. The sounds came from the direction of our lines.

It's a patrol! They've sent out a patrol from our side to see what happened up here.

Hallelujah, I've been saved! My prayers have been answered!

"Over here", I shouted in a weak voice. "I'm over here".

Oh, thank God they heard me and are coming over to save me.

"Achtung! Raus mitt!"

It was a German patrol

Someone was telling me to stand up as several rifle barrels pointed to my head.

I spoke the only German words I could think of.

"Nichts – Ich bin kaput!"

Two men then grabbed my arms and dragged me to my feet only to have me collapse in a heap when they let go.

Then the one who was obviously their leader, leaned over to my face and whispered, "Habenze Ziggarettin"

They had cleaned me out pretty good earlier in the day, but I felt around my pockets anyway. There! In my shirt pocket, I felt a bulge. It was a pack.

"Ja here" I whispered back.

With that he put his finger to pursued lips then turned and barked some orders to his men. The men took off and the squad leader returned to the task of trying to retrieve this bulge in my shirt pocket that had been missed by the earlier scavengers. He took out a large knife and cut through the bandoliers across my chest, cut through the ammo belt around my waist so he could remove the camouflage suit, worked his hand under my overcoat, then through my field jacket and finally to my shirt pocket. A pack of Lucky Strikes emerged as his bounty. Again, he put his finger up to pursued lips and stood up just as two of his men returned. They had been sent back to their lines to bring a stretcher!

And I thought they would either shoot me or merely leave me there to die a natural death by morning.

Sure hands lifted my body onto the stretcher and then carried me some distance until we reached what appeared to be an Aid Station. I lay on the floor of that Aid Station the rest of the night and most of the next day with only a curious look or two from the German medics on duty.

Chapter 4

SERENDIPITY

Lying in that Aid Station with nothing to do, I played mind games to stay awake. Why hadn't that Major at the hospital in France contacted me about that transfer to Special Services? Wouldn't that be nice? A warm bed every night without worrying about annoying things like whizzing bullets, mortar shell or tanks. Instead I could be making people happy for a little while at least.

To make people happy, to make them laugh always gave me the greatest pleasure.

It started back when I was only five. Our kindergarten class encouraged all the kids to try their hand at one of the many musical instruments they had available. There were cymbals, horns, (like a kazoo), bells, chimes, a small glockenspiel and drums. I was drawn to the glockenspiel and soon found myself playing melodies by ear. I also was picked to lead the daily "parade" around the classroom.

My teachers thought that I was quite talented and encouraged me to try different melodies. Everything came easily. The right tempo, the right notes and a good memory soon made me the "Teacher's Pet".

So much so that another boy got so jealous of my attention that he pushed me into a small gold fish pond which we had in our classroom. I got soaking wet but the teachers found something for me to wear while my clothes were drying out.

The boy's name was Shepherd Zinavoy and we later became good friends. As a matter of fact, I was his campaign manager when he ran for, and became president of the seventh grade class at DeWitt Clinton Elementary School in Mt. Vernon, N.Y.

My older brother Sudy, who was always very enterprising, made extra money by selling Liberty Magazines door-to-door. He was very good at it, and, besides earning money, he accumulated points to be redeemed for prizes. Having decided to redeem a good quantity of points, my mother helped him to pick a junior size accordion as a prize. After it arrived my brother toyed with it a short while then lost interest. Seeing my chance, I picked up that accordion one day and explored it's workings. To my surprise and satisfaction, I found it rather easy to play as I fumbled through "Mary Had a Little Lamb" and other tunes I was familiar with.

One day I brought the accordion to my kindergarten class for one of those "show-n-tell" sessions. The teachers were amazed at how well I had mastered the instrument and, before I knew it, they had convinced our principal that I should perform for the whole school.

At our next general assembly I was introduced and then stood up to play "America". Standing there on the stage in my short pants at the age of five I got my first taste of "Show

Biz" and I liked it. I liked seeing people smile, I liked the approving looks, and I liked the applause. From then on I became involved with every musical production that was ever produced during my stay in Elementary, Junior High, High School (and then, after the war, in College).

Back from my reveries, I spotted a German Medic looking at me and observing that I was shivering from the cold. He proceeded to cover me with another blanket for which I thanked him. Warming up, I settled back on my stretcher to review what had happened since the day before. Eventually my thoughts came back to that pack of Lucky Strikes and that compassionate squad leader. Unconsciously my hand went to my shirt pocket as if I would magically find another pack of Luckies to become my passport out of this place.

On the way back from my shirt pocket my hand passed over another bulge. Could it be another pack of cigarettes? The bulge was in my field jacket pocket and I was surprised to find that I still had anything left after the previous scavenging searches. I explored further, and, much to my surprise and chagrin, felt the cold, corrugated steel of a hand grenade! A hand grenade, I thought what if I get caught with it? They'll think I was hiding it for some malevolent reason. How did everyone miss such a bulky item? No matter. The thing now is what to do with it? I can't just leave it on the floor when they eventually cart me away. Someone is sure to see it and think that I planted it there. Nor can I call over an orderly and ask him for a waste basket because I have something to throw away. Besides I don't even know the German word for wastebasket. I could possibly roll it down the hall and let someone find it far from me, but the noise made by a rolling grenade would surely bring many curious investigators. Then I thought maybe one of these orderlies would like a souvenir of the war. Being stuck behind the lines they wouldn't get many opportunities to lift a memento off an enemy soldier. That's probably the best plan, I thought. Wait until another orderly comes near my stretcher and simply offer him the prize.

A short while later two Medics headed my way. They were busily engrossed in conversation as they approached. Now is my chance! I thought as I extended my arm out from under the blanket with the grenade cradled in the palm of my hand. They were so busy that they didn't see this move so I gave out a loud, "Hey!" and offered them the grenade.

Startled by this sight they stopped dead in their tracks with eyes bulging widely in fearsome disbelief. In one swift motion they both let out a scream and scampered back down the hallway as fast as they could.

I hollered, "No, come back it's OK"

They must have thought I was going to commit Hari Kari and take both of them with me. When they didn't hear an explosion, they stopped running. Peering around the corner of the hallway I saw them still with eyes bulging and chattering some unintelligible epitaphs. I waved them to come back. As they inched their way slowly and cautiously back, I could hear them calling me some very choice names none of which would have been very complimentary had I been able to understand the language.

"It's OK" I said. "Here, souvenir" and I pointed to the pull ring saying "Achtung! Nichts!

It was obvious they had never seen a G I grenade before and became extremely interested. One of them, a young chap with short, blond hair in his early twenties, took the grenade gingerly and carefully examined it with his friend. A smile broke out on their faces when they realized the humor of the situation and that I meant no harm. On the contrary, I was offering them a present. With several good chuckles and a farewell "Danka" they left to go about their business.

Evidently the word of this incident spread like wildfire because, before long, a parade of medics tramped up to my stretcher asking if I had more "Souvenirs". Much to their dismay, there was nothing else but my combat boots and no one even thought of asking for them. Evidently a soldier's boots were a sacred thing even for the enemy as I was to find out later.

Chapter 5

WHAT'S IN A NAME?

𝕝𝕝

Later that evening I was carried into a large tent, put on a table with a single lamp hanging over it. A short stocky fellow wearing what looked like a bloody butcher's apron, came over to the table, picked up the blanket over me, looked at my wounds, muttered something in German then turned to me.

"Ve haff to operate on your vounds to clean zem out und prevent infection" he said in fairly good English.

"However" he continued, "you must know zat ve do not haff any anesthetic to spare zo ve vill have to operate mit-out anesthetic. Verstehen?"

Before I had a chance to say anything, the doctor called over four burly guards with instruction to drape themselves over my chest, arms and legs so that I could not move.

Then the operation proceeded.

Totally oblivious to any possible consequences, I screamed my head off and tried to lift those goons off me. I fought with every ounce of strength as I felt each snip of scissors cutting flesh, the slicing scalpel as it made rapid cuts, the reaming action of something entering one side of my leg and coming out the other!

I screamed and cursed and found strength I never suspected I would have, after 36 hours of profound tribulation. They must have thought, "How ungrateful this poor chap is, when all we're doing is for his own good".

Then it was over. The little butcher wiped the blood from his gloved hands and told me, "Alle ist gut!"

They carried me back on a stretcher and set me down on what seemed to be the floor of a stable. It was not long before a German officer came in with a stool, set it down next to me and sat down while taking a little pad and pencil out of his pocket.

"How are you feeling?" He asked in perfect English. "We want to ask you a few questions".

Oh boy, I thought, here it comes. The interrogation that we were trained to expect if we were ever captured. Name, rank and serial number – that's all you have to give according to the Geneva Convention.

"Are you hungry/" came the next question.

He's trying to butter me up, I thought.

But without an answer he handed me a slab of black bread covered with smalz (chicken fat). Of course I accepted it greedily not having had anything to eat for almost two days!

"Incidentally" he slipped in "what was the name of your outfit?"

"My name is Vahan Hovhannissian, serial number 32804738, my rank is ...." But he cut me off with a curt "We know who you are from your dog tags. By the way, what kind of a name is that? Your first name could be Jewish but the last name… is it Syrian?"

"No" I replied, "that's a 100% Armenian name".

"Oh Armenian, yes, they are good people. I think they suffered much from the Turks, yes?"

"Yes, very much. The Turks massacred over 3,000,000 Armenians" I confirmed, "even part of my family was killed by the Turks". Most Germans were aware of the Armenian Massacres because Adolph Hitler had referred to them in his book *Meine Kampf*, pointing out that the world has basically forgotten what the Turks have done as they will forget what we must do (the Jewish question).

"Do you know that soldier next to you?" he asked.

I looked over and saw, for the first time, another soldier lying on a stretcher behind mine. I recognized him immediately as a buddy from my platoon. His name was Max Friedman but I denied that I knew him. Just about then Max opened his eyes, saw me and muttered "Hey Hovey (my nickname) what are they doing to us?'

"I thought you didn't know him" snapped the officer. "No matter, he has already told us that you are from Company C of the 66th AIB (Armored Infantry Battalion)".

I neither agreed nor disagreed. I just clammed up and silently cursed Max for his big mouth. The interview ended as quickly as it started. After a few minutes two Orderlies came in, picked up my stretcher and carried me out into the night. I was then lifted up and placed in what turned out to be a horse drawn cart or wagon. I looked around for Max, or perhaps, some other G.I.s, but no one else was put on the wagon. I was completely alone and could only imagine what happened to my buddy Max.

With my head near the driver's bench I watched as he picked up the reins and snapped them on the horse's back to get him started. It was a rickety ride wherein every bump was unceremoniously announced to my aching back and my freshly bandaged legs. Soon, however, I could hear the sound of bubbling water and that certain hollow sound as we clacked along, like crossing some kind of bridge. We must be on a bridge crossing the Rhine, I thought, for I knew the

Rhine River was just beyond the Hagenau Woods. But then, about half way over the bridge, the wagon stopped with a universal "Whoa".

Here it comes. I thought. They're all finished with me and they told my driver to go over the bridge and dump this guy in the river – he's only in our way.

But the driver reached under his coat, pulled out a flask and took a nice big swig followed by a satisfying "Aaah!"

He then looked down at my wondering eyes and, holding out the flask asked, "Schanpps?"

I never was much of a drinker and I had never tasted Schnapps before but I figured "What the Hell. I'm freezing; they're probably going to do away with me anyway, so, why not?"

I reached for the flask, took a hearty swig and felt the wild fire race down my throat, spread like searing fingers throughout my chest and finally settle down to some serious burning in my stomach. With a bulgy-eyed gasp I managed a weak "Danka" and watched as the smiling old man wiped the flask on his sleeve before taking another healthy swallow.

With that kind, smiling face etched in my mind, I either passed out from weakness, fell asleep, or, passed out dead drunk as we proceeded over the bridge.

The next thing I remember was waking up in a military ambulance that eventually stopped at the admitting door of what seemed to be a very fancy hospital.

Chapter 6

ON WITH THE SHOW!

I t didn't take very long to realize that this was no ordinary hospital. As I gazed at the picture-lined hallways, elegant light fixtures, well dressed nurses, orderlies and doctors busily darted from room to room charts in hand, incessantly chattering among themselves. Only an occasional glance my way from anyone as they rolled my gurney to a fairly large room containing four beds. After being lifted onto my bed I was immediately surrounded by several nurses. With their crisp, starched uniforms crackling with every move, and typically business-like German efficiency, they proceeded to remove my remaining clothing. I was given a sponge bath and settled back in my bed with a clean new hospital gown. I was afraid to open my mouth up to this point because I just couldn't believe that an American P.O.W. could be entitled to such treatment.

"Du bist Amerikaner" asked the patient alongside me.

So the word is out that I'm American but where's the hostility?

"Ja" I replied, but that was the end of our conversation because the only response I could give to a barrage-of-questions from him and the other two patients was "Nichts Verstehen"

Lunch time came and my tray was the same as everyone else. The nurse even cranked up my bed, fluffed my pillow and admonished me to "Essen!" What is this place? I thought. Did I die and go to P.O.W. heaven? Did someone make a mistake and take me for some V.I.P.?

Am I going to be a guinea pig for some of those weird experiments that the Germans are known for?

Well, I was soon going to learn that one of those theories was pretty close to the answer.

The next Gurney ride from my room was to reveal more of the opulence I observed upon arrival. An elevator ride exited on a floor with quite a different ambiance. Tiled walls, shiny marble floors, overhead inset lights and groups of doctors huddled together talking over charts and reports.

The room I ended up in looked like an operating room with a battery of lights over the center table, equipment, tubes, oxygen tanks, x-ray machines and various medical paraphernalia. I was immediately surrounded by a group of doctors and nurses who proceeded to cut away my bandages in order to get at my wounds.

Then the head nurse, a gorgeous statuesque woman with short cropped hair and beautiful hazel eyes, spoke to me in perfect English. "Well soldier, for you it looks like the war is over. Do not be frightened, the doctors must examine and care for your wounds", she purred.

"Wow", I asked "Where did you come from? Why are you here? Where am I? What's going to happen?"

Actually my name is Frieda and I was born and brought up in a little town outside of Cleveland, Ohio. My parents are German and I was sent here to study nursing before the war broke out. When that happened I thought it would be patriotic to stay here and help the people of my heritage. And now, I must stay because they need me too much?

The head doctor interrupted our conversation by issuing some orders. One of the nurses took a strip of bandage that she fashioned into a small sling. Then she slipped this sling under my testicles and lifted them up as high as she could. Several doctors then peered into that area vacated by my testicles and a lively discussion erupted among them. Several other young doctors were invited to also take a look with more discussion.

What's going on Frieda? Is something wrong?"

"No" she replied, "the doctors are amazed at your wounds".

"Why? I have no idea what happened" I shot back.

"Well it seems that a bullet entered your left leg and then struck your thigh bone, turned and exited your leg sideways. Then it entered your other leg sideways and exited the other side flattened out".

"So, what's so strange about that?" I asked.

"The thing that puzzles the doctors is that where the bullet came out of one leg and then entered the other left – that's where your testicles are? That which is amazing to the doctors is how that bullet hit your bone without breaking it, how it missed major arteries in each leg, and, how your …er.. private parts escaped being hit!"

"That's easy" I explained with the bravado of a stage magician, "the bone didn't break because Armenians are known for strong bones due to all the homemade yogurt we eat. And the bullet that could have made me a Eunuch was directed on its path by a certain guiding hand".

"Whose hand?" She asked.

"The Hand of God" I replied with a smile on my face.

She translated all of this to the group assembled. I heard a chuckle when she told them about the yogurt, but a serious silence with only nodding heads when she told them about "The Hand of God".

While the doctors were treating and dressing my wounds, they continued a lively discussion with other doctors that came and went during the procedure. Nurse Frieda told me "You are in one of the finest Spa Hotels in Baden Baden which has been converted as a special teaching hospital. Here they bring special cases that require unique attention and are used to expose new doctors to the treatments required for proper cure. I can only guess that you were sent here because of the extraordinary nature of your wounds".

"Will you go back to Ohio after the war?" I probed.

"Probably not" she replied, "I hope to settle down and raise a family here in Germany after the war is over".

Back in my room I lay back with closed eyes and wondered about the extraordinary good luck that had befallen me. Or was it just luck? Hadn't Reverend Houghton back in my church in Mt. Vernon taught us that there really isn't a thing called "luck". "Everything in your life happens because of God's Master Plan" he would preach. "What most people call luck is really the Grace of God. If it is His will for you to be in an accident, or just miss having one by just a fraction of a second, for example – that's not plain 'luck' but the Grace of God influencing your life".

And for that we must ever be thankful and full of praise for a loving God who watches over his flock like the good shepherd.

The nurse brought in an in-between-meal snack which she doled out to everyone in the room. It was a slab of blood-wurst, I believe made from cow's blood. We were also given a glass of red wine which instantly brought to mind a passage from the 23rd Psalm – "and You prepare a table before me even in the face of my enemies…"

I was later told that German Hospitals were almost completely out of blood plasma. So, the next best thing that they could do for men who lost a lot of blood was to have a daily ration of blood-wurst and a glass of red wine. Evidently they believed that this combination would help the body produce new blood at a faster rate.

It must have worked because I could feel myself getting stronger for each of the five days that I was at Baden Baden. Or, perhaps it was the thought of maybe seeing Frieda again that sent waves of energy through my body. In any case, the powers that be decided I was strong enough to move on.

Chapter 7

GOTT IST GUT!

The ambulance was a short ride to the railway station where sure hands picked up my stretcher and gingerly carried me through a rail car that was already laden with wounded soldiers. The stretchers were stacked three or four deep like tiers of a big bunk bed. My stretcher was placed on a top rack very close to the ceiling of the rail car. It was not until then that I noticed how very careful the German medics were to place your shoes and other personal belongings right at the foot of your stretcher. In any case, all I had was my combat boots which faithfully followed me wherever I went. Of course, the sight of American combat boots were a dead giveaway that I was not one of them, causing many curious glances and inquisitive comments. Nevertheless it was gratifying to see that I was being given the same care and attention as all the other wounded. Still, I did not see any other non-Germans. I felt strangely privileged to be the only Allied P.O.W. in the midst of the enemy right in their own back yard, so to speak.

It was a rather long and tediously slow trip on that train, making many stops along the way – presumably to take on more wounded. It was not until the next day that we arrived at the town of Donaeshegan. From the station there was another ambulance ride to Reserve Lazarette Donaeshegan. I was later to learn that Reserve Lazarette, or Res. Laz as it was abbreviated, was the official designation for a Military Hospital.

I was placed in a large ward this time on a cot next to the cot of another patient. Again, I saw nothing but German patients and soldiers, not a single Allied soldier like myself.

I was greeted by the usual examination followed by a series of doctors and nurses peering at my wounds. Then came the usual occasional words of amazement or whistles of disbelief. As in Baden Baden, I soon became the local "freak show" that all the curious had to come and see. I quite often thought – Gee, if only I could sell tickets – I could make a fortune! "Step right up and see Hovey's privates – one of the wonders of the war!"

By now, however, my attention and the attention of my attending physicians, was turned to my hands and feet. They had been frozen during my ordeal on the battlefield and were now slowly thawing out. I was experiencing an extremely painful tingling – especially in my feet. An English speaking doctor told me that, as the circulation slowly comes back to my feet, I can expect the skin to dry out and fall off the bottom of my feet (like a snake shedding it's skin). And so it was - every day they looked at my feet, checked for feeling, the peeling and drying out. In a few days skin started peeling off in fairly large pieces leaving skin behind that was super sensitive even to the touch of the bed sheets. The tingling pain grew almost unbearable at times but there was nothing to be done, especially since I was in no position to complain to anyone.

Without anything to read or anyone to converse with I turned to the only true friend I had. "Dear Jesus, please help me stand this pain. Please restore my hands so that I can continue to play the piano. Please do not let gangrene set into my feet because I know the consequence of that! I put myself completely in your hands and ask for full healing".

"The Lord is my shepherd, I shall not want...."

Yes, I said it over and over again and it eased the pain! No, the tingling didn't stop, but the awful pain that came with it no longer seemed to bother me. Every day it got a little less and less until about the fourth day of my stay there, I turned by attention to the soldier next to me.

His name was Hans Erlich and he had made several attempts to talk to me ever since I was placed next to him (literally elbow to elbow). He must have understood what I was going through because he would always smile at me and occasionally reach over and pat my shoulder gently. Hans couldn't speak a word of English, nor I any German, but we started to communicate. I ascertained that he had a wife and two children and that he lived on a farm with his mother. He must have been in his middle forties and had been in the army since 1939. A husky fellow with reddish-blond hair, blue eyes sunk into a weather beaten face and large, calloused hands. His deep voice would almost thunder when he laughed and it soon became apparent that he was the Joker in the ward. Every once in a while he would be telling the other patients something and then they would all break out in laughter. Several times he tried to tell me a joke with sign language and a few words that we had in common (I found out that German is very much like English) and he would make me laugh. Not necessarily at the joke but the way he was trying to explain it to me. Once, Hans observed me praying and he gently asked me, "Gott in Himmel?"

"Yes" I replied. "My God is good to me".

"Ja, Gott ist gut. Due Bist O.K." he hurried to say. Hans soon let the other patients know that not only was I an American but that I was an Armenian and a Christian. This seemed to please most everyone there and I was happy to see that the atheistic culture proposed by the Third Reich was not as pervasive as most people thought.

Evidently Donaeshegan was a favorite target for Allied bombers judging by the frequency that air raid sirens wailed their mournful warning. On each occasion, all ambulatory patients would scurry downstairs and those that couldn't were patiently carried down on stretchers. Beneath our hospital was a catacomb of underground rooms with arched ceilings. It reminded me of a huge wine cellar or perhaps a secret dungeon that I had seen in some Hollywood movie. Fortunately, for me I was taken down with everyone else. The obvious thought that came to me was why they didn't just leave me there to suffer the consequences that were brought on by planes from my side. Nevertheless, the second raid I experienced was the worst. Living through an air raid is probably right up there in the top ten of frightening experiences! Deep in the bowels of the earth you have no idea of what to expect next. A distant rumbling like thunder grows louder and louder as the wave of terror comes closer and closer to where you are. Then, the unbearable din and fearsome earth-trembling that makes you think that the bombs are surely right over your head. Dust and pieces of plaster came raining down as the single-bulb ceiling lights flickered and swayed in disorderly cadence. And the screams! Grown men, hardened veterans of ghastly campaigns started wailing and screaming…some for their mothers (meine mutti!) some for their nurses (sonnie, sonnie) and just a few for their God (meine Gott, meine Gott!). I thought this must surely be the end as I found myself uttering "Though I walk through the valley of the shadow of death, I will fear no evil for you are with me…"

And so he was.

After the raid they started carrying us back upstairs to what? Surely the hospital could not have survived that terrible concentration of horror. As we got back to my ward I thought I must truly be seeing a miracle. Strangely, nothing seemed to be any different than when we went downstairs. Sure there were broken windows but the roof was still intact and so were all the rooms. Had our bombers been so good as to miss this building on purpose? Sure, there was a big Red

Cross painted on the roof, as was the custom on both sides, but there had to be more. Some force, some invisible hand directed bombs away from this hospital building. It had to be—The Hand of God!

Thank you Lord. Thank you for your loving hand. Thank you for hearing my prayers!

About a week later I was shipped out again. Before leaving, however, I exchanged home addresses with Hans amid promises that we would keep in touch after the war. As it turned out, he did write first about a year after the armistice, asking for clothes—anything—new or used. He said they were having a very tough time and needed clothing and food most of all. My parents helped me to accumulate a large box of clothing and some canned goods. The box was rather heavy so we shipped it by boat. Hans thankfully received it about three months later and immediately acknowledged his gratitude in a letter. (Fortunately, we had a neighbor who was able to translate his letters.) The letters stopped after a while and I never really found out why.

Chapter 8

HELGA

❧

My destination this time was the well-equipped Res. Laz. Konstanz, a very picturesque, typically Bavarian style building in Konstanz, a small resort town situated on the Swiss border right on Lake Konstanz. It had been a fairly short ride by military ambulance through a pastoral countryside that didn't look like it had been touched by the war. I was carried to a semi-private room and placed in a bed next to the window. From that vantage point I could see the lake with small boats sailing back and forth to a picture-postcard waterfront complete with its quaint little shops. Across the lake was a range of snow-capped mountains that protectively embraced the lake like a mother hen watching over her brood. I was soon to find out that what I was viewing was Switzerland. Oh, if I could only let myself down a rope from this window and fall into one of those little boats, I could sail that short distance to freedom and safety. Then I would sit back, relax and watch the world go by till the war was over. It soon became evident, however, that I was about to do the same thing right where I was (for a little while anyhow).

This hospital was more like a convalescent hospital from the others I came from. The staff seemed to be mostly civilian as opposed to military personnel. I underwent the usual bandage changing and the wide-eyed gawking as one after another doctor or nurse would come in to see the wonder of my wounds.

The German soldier in my room must have been in rather serious condition because he never spoke to me or to the staff. He was either asleep or unconscious a good deal of the time. His head was swathed in a very large bandage which they changed every day. I couldn't tell his age because of the unshaved face that was half covered by bandage. I guessed he was somewhere between 35 and 40.

More refreshing than the pastoral view out my window however, was the bundle of sunshine that bounced into my room every morning bright and early. It was Helga, a young fraulein with golden hair that fell in two long braids over her shoulders and down her well-endowed bosom. Her blue eyes, which looked green at times, sparkled with the joy of teenage exuberance. A slightly freckled face always wore a pleasant smile that accompanied her usual, sing-song "Gutte Morgan!".

From the first day I arrived, I noticed Helga showing me an unusual amount of attention. She didn't know a word of English and I very little German—but we got along very well. She so much wanted to learn English and the words came rather easily to her alert mind. How she would stare at my lips as I pronounced my words. Then she reproduced the sound perfectly even without knowing what the word meant. It was a memorable experience exchanging my words for hers and vice versa. We both learned a great deal about each other's language and a great deal about each other.

Helga's family lived there in Konstanz and operated a little shop. I never could understand what they did but it didn't matter. Her older brother had been killed in the war just before Christmas and that was still heavy on her heart. She showed me his picture in uniform and we held hands and said a prayer for him. The tears streamed down her face as I assured her that he must surely be in heaven smiling down on us in complete peace.

As the days went by we got closer and closer. Helga would stay in my room after the daily sponge bath and talk to me. She showed me more pictures of her family, asked about my family, asked if I had a girlfriend back home. But the biggest wonderment was her immense fascination with New York City. She would ask as to how big it was, what could one do there, how tall are the buildings, how about the Statue of Liberty, the night life, the shops. I finally resorted to drawing pictures of skyscrapers and little cars and people to show their comparative sizes. She was enraptured with every single detail and the more she learned the more questions she asked.

One day I took Helga's hand and told her fortune by reading the lines. I had learned a little about palm reading from the mother of the girl I knew back in High School. I told her she would have a long life, that her heart would dominate the decisions in her life, that she was musically inclined and, that she would have at least three kids. This all amazed her so that she went out to tell her co-worker friends. What a mistake that was!

The steady parade of nurses, nurse's aids, patients and others kept me busy for hours. I soon became known throughout the hospital as the American Fortune Teller! Step right up, no waiting! At least it was a show with a little more class than the one I had contemplated earlier.

Telling fortunes helped me learn the language faster and it helped dispel any dislike that they had for Americans. The first question I was usually asked when a German discovered I was an American "Fleiger?"

As soon as they found out I was not a pilot everything was O.K. and the hand of friendship would be extended. The civilians especially hated pilots because almost everyone had a loved one or friend that was either killed or maimed during a bombing raid.

Food was meager, meat was almost non-existent. Lots of potatoes, vegetables and again, blood-wurst. One thing that struck me as strange from my days at Donaeshegan, every soldier was issued a ration of beer every single day. Without fail, an orderly would come around in the middle of the afternoon and give you a bottle of beer! Of course, I was always included and I soon looked forward to that daily ritual even though the beer was never cold. Most Europeans, in fact, drink their beer room temperature not ice cold as we like it in the U.S.

I thought back to my hospital stay in France and remembered that our boys usually got regular free rations of chocolate bars and cigarettes. Both of these goodies became valuable bartering tools for goods and services throughout France and Germany. I felt sorry, in a way, that the Germans didn't have that pleasure but then, they did have their daily beer which we didn't.

Nine days after I had arrived at Res. Laz. Konstanz, I was moved once again. Early on the morning of February 11, 1945, Helga came in for the customary ablutions but something was different. No bubbly greeting, no sunshiny smile, no bounce to her step. Only a sad face.

"Vas ist loss?" I asked.

That did it. The dam burst and a torrent of tears rained down on my chest as she embraced with abandon. If he was conscious, my roommate paid no attention to the uncontrolled sobbing. Between the outpourings she managed to inform me that her world was coming to an end because I was to be shipped out that same day.

As I lay on a stretcher by the loading dock waiting to be put in an ambulance, a tearful Helga came by my side to say goodbye. She wanted to know if I would come back to see her after the war. And, more important, she made me promise that I would take her to America to see New York City. What else could I do or say. Of course, I would try to come back, and of course, I would whisk her off to see New York City.

Helga bent over my stretcher and, with a furtive glance either way; she unfolded her apron to reveal three or four green apples. She tucked them under my blanket with strict instructions that I eat them on my journey. I thanked her. We hugged an awkward hug and kissed an awkward kiss as orderlies picked up my stretcher and placed me in the ambulance. I could still see her water-logged face as she stood there waving a little embroidered handkerchief. They closed the doors and slowly drove away. I never saw Helga again.

Chapter 9

THE SCENIC ROUTE

B ack again on a train, I found myself comparatively alone. This was not a military troop or hospital train. Evidently, I was in what appeared to be a baggage car of a civilian train. There were a few other stretchers but not where I could see them. The train seemed to make many stops and traveled rather slowly. When the big sliding door was occasionally opened I would catch glimpses of mountains in the distance. Under any other conditions, this could certainly be called a Scenic Tour. Workers in the fields, a few cows peacefully grazing, a wisp of smoke spiraling upward from a little vine-covered cottage, flowers, trees and greenery everywhere. What a wonderfully peaceful place, I thought. How could these people want to disturb this God-given serenity and make war on their neighbors?

Any cameo glimpse would have made a perfect picture postcard except I would be hard pressed to tell anyone "wish you were here". Perhaps another time when sanity replaces greed and Godliness replaced Evil.

We arrived at Res. Laz. Rosenheim the following day. Like Konstanz, I could see very little evidence of a war going on. A short ride in an ambulance brought us to the military hospital. There the charm and serenity of Konstanz gave way to the crisp efficiency of clicking boots. Again, I was placed in a ward with German soldiers, only this time, I discovered an English speaking patient as well. He turned out to be an Englishman who was shot down some five or six months before. As a Bombardier, he was lying on his stomach fixing his sight during a raid when an anti-aircraft shell exploded beneath his plane. Several large pieces of shrapnel tore into his stomach as other pieces evidently crippled his plane. He managed to crawl, or was pulled back to an open hatch as the crew abandoned the doomed aircraft. He remembered waking up in a German hospital but didn't remember how he got there. The doctors had to remove a good part of his intestines and his colon forcing the poor chap to wear a bag strapped around his wrist. This bag caught his daily excrements and although he was still alive, the routine of emptying the bag with its accompanying odors was rather unpleasant to say the least. The procedure he underwent was called a colostomy and little did I know that I would have the exact same thing many years later because of a ruptured Diverticula.

We exchanged names and addresses not knowing how long we would be together. Although we never corresponded after the war, I did remember his name – Dudley Pearson and he was from Surrey, England.

The care at Rosenheim was quite good. The doctors made daily rounds in their crisp German uniforms and brightly shining boots. There were no female nurses, only male orderlies who saw to all our needs quite nicely.

Again the "Hovey Show 'N Tell" was the highlight of our ward. There was even one doctor who took measurements and plotted angles on a chart with some puzzling conclusions.

"Impossible! That you are still a man. Impossible!" He would mutter in very good English. According to the angle of entry, there was no way that a bullet could follow the course that mine did without causing some measure of castration. Nevertheless, there I was – in one piece and recovering very nicely! Thanks to the Doctors at Baden Baden, my wounds were dressed in such a way as to allow the healing to occur from inside to outside. As it was explained to me, there would have to be considerable drainage during the healing process. To allow for this, the wounds had to be kept open until all the infection and drainage had run its course. Had the bullet holes closed up on the surface as they would be naturally prone to do, the drainage would have no escape route and serious complications could set in. I have been told many times by many physicians that I am extremely lucky that the Germans treated my wounds as they did. Lucky? Perhaps.

But I like to think that the hands that treated me were guided by the greatest of all healing hands – the Hand of God!

Nothing very eventful happened at Res. Laz. Rosenheim. There was occasional wailing of air raid sirens but never any bombings on our town. The planes would just fly over the town toward some other target to deposit their lethal cargo of destruction. I thought often of Helga, then again, I also thought of Frieda, and what about Virginia who I left at the train station in Mt. Vernon. Mostly pleasant thoughts helped pass away the seven days that I stayed at Rosenheim.

Chapter 10

FREISING

This time I found myself in an ambulance on a stretcher next to one occupied by Dudley Pearson.

"Know where we're going?" I asked him.

"I think they are sending us to a Stalag (P.O.W. Camp)" he replied.

That's strange I thought. Neither one of us could walk and we're going to end up in Stalag with barracks and barbed wire and all that stuff. Three or so hours later our ambulance struggled and whined its way up some steep road to finally stop at a large, mustard color building inside a walled courtyard.

"Hey Dudley" I remarked, "This ain't no Stalag!"

"You're right mate. Let's take it as it comes".

We arrived at Res. Laz. Freising, a P.O.W. hospital approximately 20 kilometers north of Munich. It was a typical Bavarian village with narrow cobblestone streets, multi-colored houses with their mandatory flower boxes, little cars darting about and a clanking trolley rumbling down the street. The men, mostly elderly, wore knickered pants or long pants with that shiny leathery look. And the women with their apron-like dresses or knickers under a tweed jacket topped with a feathered felt hat. The courtyard we entered was part of a small monastic cloister wherein resided Nuns of an uncertain order. (I never found out what order).

The Nuns wore bluish gray habits covered by a wide starched apron. Their headdress fanned out at the sides like the tail fins of a 1949 Cadillac. The second floor of this convent had been transformed into a medical hospital to care for wounded prisoners of war. There were two very large rooms – one devoted to Allied P.O.W.s (about 50 in all) and the other room reserved for Russian P.O.W.s (about 100). The Allied ward was attended by an American Doctor who had been captured early in the war and pressed into this service. His name was Dr. Lawrence E. Kramer and I believe he came from the Boston area. It was his duty to tend to all the wounded, keep records of each patient and to report each one's progress to the German army doctor who made regular rounds once a week. It was on the German doctor's first round since I got there that the Oberarzt's attention was drawn to my peculiar wounds. He observed for quite a while, made notes and, thereafter, made it a special point to follow my progress.

The patient mix in our room was made up of an equal amount of British and Americans. Everyone wore his own uniform (there was no prison garb for us) or, as in my case, a hospital nightshirt and bathrobe. Somehow there was a ready supply of extra uniforms for those that required it. After I finally started walking with crutches, a clean set of Olive Drabs were given to me from our "supply room".

Both the British and the Americans were extra fortunate in that we would receive a Red Cross Parcel once a month. That the Germans let them go through to us is still a mystery to me for each parcel contained goodies like cigarettes, candy, gum, writing paper, pen, k-rations and other basic necessities. Except when the German doctor was there you would think that you were back in the States in some American Hospital surrounded by buddies and friends that were truly comrades. The Russians, on the other hand, who were crowded into another room about the same size as ours, had nothing. They all wore prison-type striped pajamas, all their heads were shaved during the de-licing procedure and they were all very thin. They had no doctor in attendance only the weekly visit by the Oberarzt who seemed to whisk through their ward with amazing dispatch. The sisters of the cloister prepared and served – once a day – a hot soup made from potato skins and, occasionally a slice of black bread. That was the only thing the Russians had for sustenance. No wonder they were so thin! At least we had our Red Cross parcel to supplement this meager ration of soup.

Red Cross Parcel time was a little like Christmas. We would open our boxes like anticipating kids even though we knew what was inside. Many of the guys would swap or share some of their goodies with someone else. Cigarettes, for example, became the most valuable thing in the parcel. Cigarettes and chocolate were like money. You could buy almost anything with them if the price were right. We often played Poker using cigarettes as money. Fortunately, I was a steady winner and managed to accumulate a hoard of cigarettes. Smoking them was out of the question. I would buy someone's k-ration can, or chocolate bar or send someone down to the guard at the front door and bribe him to smuggle us some apples.

There were no orderlies or nurses tending to our needs so I had to depend on my buddies to empty my bed pan when necessary. Quite often even the lure of the extra cigarettes wasn't enough to entice one of my buddies to take on this messy job. Then, one day, I saw two Russian P.O.W.s standing outside the archway to our ward. They were enviously looking at the well-fed guys playing around and obviously in very little distress. But wait. They were not talking in Russian – they were conversing in Armenian! I quickly called out to them in Armenian to come in – "I'm Armenian too!"

They were so astounded that they just froze there with open mouths.

"You are Armenian?" one of them finally raised his voice to ask.

"Yes, I assured them "come in, come in"

Hesitatingly they edged their way toward my bunk. I told the boys nearby "they're OK. I invited them in" (we never associated with the Russians and they were told not to enter our ward).

It turned out that these two "Russians" were Armenians who had been conscripted into the Russian Army. We talked about many things as they shared a chocolate bar I offered them. Dikran, who lived outside of Moscow, was the shorter man's name and he had been swept into the army at an early age. He had been through many campaigns as his war-torn face reflected. A bad case of Trench foot had brought him to Freising. Levon, on the other hand, came from Armenia which was Sovietized back in 1922 after a brief 2-year taste of independence. He was considerably younger and had been in the army only a few months when they sent him to the Front where he was wounded, captured and then eventually brought to Freising.

Understanding each other was not very easy as they both talked rapidly and with an accent I was not familiar with. I also found myself groping for words I had either forgotten or never had in my vocabulary. Nevertheless, we plodded through the "pleasantries" amid the gawking stares of my buddies, several of whom remarked, "We didn't know you spoke Russian"

As we were talking, an idea began to germinate in my head that I was almost too embarrassed to propose. I told them of my dilemma in finding someone to empty my bed pan after I had used it. I suggested that I would be willing to pay either one of them (or both) to empty my bed pan as needed. The idea did not sit too well with Dikran, especially when I offered as payment two cigarettes for each emptying.

Levon, however jumped at the chance and the deal was sealed. I gave them each a cigarette as they left which they declined to light right away but opted to smoke later on. From then on, Levon would come by every day to see if I needed his services and, before long, several of my buddies employed his services on the same basis. Levon soon became a V.I.P. among his comrades many of who ventured to the entrance of our ward hoping to find similar employment or favors.

Chapter 11

NEVER SAY NEVER

Day to day life at Freising settled down to a predictable routine. Daily visits by our doctor, bandage changes, reading or writing, card playing, weekly inspection by our German Oberarzt and window watching when you could get to one. Every day, it seemed, air raid sirens would sound the alert in town and soon after the thunderous drone of B-17 Superfortress Bombers would fill the air. Any one who could get to a window would watch as these graceful formations would majestically glide overhead as their finger-like vapor trails etched a billowy highway that many more would follow. Because Freising had never been bombed so far in the war, none of the townspeople seemed to pay attention to the possible danger above. It was business as usual as people continued on their with only an occasional glance skyward. American planes would pass over daily on their way to plaster Munich. A short while after the planes were out of sight a series of dull thuds signaled that the payload deposits had been made on target. Then, the planes would return home via a different route.

"Go give them hell!" we would all shout "let 'em have it good!" As we cheered them on. Later, on several occasions, we were admonished to stay away from the windows as the planes passed over because the neighbors complained about our cheering and the possibility existed that one of us could get hurt.

Then one day in April, 1945, we were watching the planes overhead as usual amidst the wailing sirens, we all heard that tell-tale whistling of falling bombs! Before anyone could react, a large explosion shook our building and the force of a shock wave knocked me right off the top tier of a bunk bed I was on. By this time I had recovered to the point where I was hobbling around on two crutches. As everyone scrambled for the stairway to seek refuge in the basement, I picked myself off the floor and proceeded to make my way to the stairway. It felt like bombs were falling all around us as the shock waves kept trying to knock me off balance. With dogged determination I managed to hobble, slide, and bounce – I don't remember which – down to the basement. There I found everyone huddled against the walls – some moaning, some quiet, some praying. I spotted one of the Nuns that served us the potato soup huddled on a bench against a wall. I went over to her and pressed my body over hers leaning against the wall as close as I could get. The building continued to shake and quiver amid the constant roar of bombs exploding all around us.

"Dear God" I prayed, "have I come this far only to be done in by my own planes?" Then I remembered – "Though I walk through the valley of the shadow of death, I will fear no evil for thou art with me…"

The bombing was over in about fifteen minutes but I still had my body cozied up flat against the wall. It was only in the uncertain quiet that I became aware of a sobbing figure that my body was practically suffocating. I pulled away only to have two desperate hands grab me and pull me back to the wall. I gently pulled away again and took the Nun's hand, patted it and assured her "it's all right". She didn't understand the words, of course, but the feeling and the reassurance got through to her. She blessed herself, then me while uttering her own prayer of thanksgiving in German. She then stood up, brushed off her habit, gave me a big hug and with a tearful "Danka" scurried off to do whatever she thought she had to do.

Climbing up the stairs in my still weak condition was not easy but with the help of a buddy, I managed to get back to my bunk. News about the bombing trickled in from sources I'm not sure of. It seems that our hospital did not suffer any direct hits at all! The closest bomb was the first that blew me off the bunk. That bomb landed just six yards outside our front door killing the old man on guard there. Besides the shattered glass, there didn't seem to be any damage to our building whatsoever!

Again, it was either expert marksmanship by our bombardiers, or, it was that invisible hand of protection once again – the Hand of God!

Although Friezing had never been bombed throughout the entire war, that good fortune came to an abrupt end that bright, sunny day. It seems that 80% of the town was demolished in this one raid which was probably designed to "soften up" the town prior to an impending assault by ground forces.

Our spirits were very high. First because we had been spared the fate of the general population and second, we knew the Allied troops would most likely be arriving soon. The only downside was the possibility that we would all be evacuated to another location as our troops advanced. Three days later this fear was put to rest. Our doctor had been informed by the German Oberarzt that he would no longer be visiting our hospital and, as far as he knew, there were no plans to evacuate. There was no place else to go! The Americans were pushing in from the West and the Russians from the East. The end had to be just a matter of days!

Chapter 12

OLD GLORY

About a week later, again came the screaming sirens from town. What's this... another bombing? We all scurried to the cellar once again as the bursting of explosions rocked the building and shook the ground. Although similar to an air raid, these explosions were less intense and only slightly less frightening. An Artillery barrage was coming in to prepare the way for foot soldiers soon to follow. No sooner did the barrage stop but we could hear the unmistakable clanking of tanks roaming through the streets indiscriminatingly firing their 75 mm cannon at suspicious targets. Then machine gun fire mixed in with all the clatter and roaring engines as they struggled up our hill.

It was late afternoon when everything turned quiet. I was seated on a bench next to a small door that led out to the lower courtyard. I slowly opened the door to see what was going on amid admonitions to be careful lest our troops mistake us for the enemy. The creaky wooden door swung open to a sight similar to one seen by Francis Scott Key once before. Across from the hill whereon stood our cloister was another hill with a government building, probably the city hall. As my door swung open I quickly called everyone around to come see the sight. There against the brilliant amber sky of late April sunset was a flagpole silhouetted against the fiery heavens. Our eyes were riveted on the sight of an American flag – Old Glory – being slowly raised to the top where it flapped and waved its ceremonial message – Freising was taken!

The cheers, the tears, the hugging, the unbelieving stares and yes, the prayers. "Thank you Lord" I said out loud, "Thank You, Thank You, Thank You".

Throttling my emotions for a few seconds, I spotted Levon standing with a group of Russians, just staring at us wondering what the excitement was all about. I yelled to him in Armenian that "WE are all free! The Americans are here! We have been freed!"

Only after translating to his comrades did the word spread amongst them. Then, they too joined in hugging and merry-making. The only somber faces to be seen were the Nuns. They too realized with mixed emotions what had happened as they solemnly withdrew to their quarters.

The first G.I.s of the 103rd Infantry Division came bursting in the front door shouting "anybody here?"

They didn't have to wait long for an answer as they were inundated by rushing figures, kissing and hugging them, shaking hands, dancing or jumping up and down around the men, asking questions and shouting "Thank You" over and over again. Eventually an Officer arrived and tried to restore some order. In order to properly sort out our situation and those of the Russians, we were told to stay put in our building until further orders. Arrangements had to be made for an orderly evacuation and there was, after all, still a war going on. We were told that the German army had deserted the town after the air raid leaving it, for all intensive purposes, up for grabs to anyone who wanted it. Unfortunately, they hadn't told that to the Allies. If they had, the Artillery barrage, the shooting up of the town by our tanks would all have been unnecessary.

The next day we were all allowed to wander through the town on a sight seeing tour. The buildings still standing were quaint, typically Bavarian in style, very neat and orderly. Gingerbread carving around the eaves, the mandatory flower boxes and various colored stucco walls with oak trim. A few townspeople were out cleaning up debris, sweeping the sidewalks or patching roofs. Most of the people stayed indoors as a mixture of P.O.W.s, G.I.s, jeeps and trucks milled about their town breathing life back into it.

Three days later all the American and British walking wounded were herded onto trucks and transported to a big open field. There we saw neat rows of C-47 transport planes and groups of army tents that have been hastily put up.

Everyone was processed as to organization, health, status of wounds, etc. Then you were assigned to a tent for bunking. You were also given toilet articles, towels, soap and any articles of clothing you were in need of. The next day brought a series of medical examinations and evaluations for travel fitness. Without wasting too much time, everything was organized and executed in a very efficient manner. It seemed that we had some type of priority being P.O.W.s The next day we boarded various C-47s according to our destination. Mine happened to be LaHavre where I was immediately put on a Liberty Ship along with other P.O.W.s.

The trip back to the States was far worse than the one going over in the first place, and that was no picnic. Going over, our outfit was assigned to an old four smoke stacked liner called The Empress of Australia. It was a British ship which must have been resurrected from a scrap heap after the war started. It was so bad that we were not allowed to board the ship in New York Harbor because the Health Department condemned the ship due to rats and other vermin. Since there was no one else available, our company received the honor of going on the ship to clean it up before the rest of our division could board. I had a suspicion that we might be in trouble with this ship when I discovered a plaque on the main deck which read, "IN HONOR OF THE VALIANT RESCUE WORK DONE DURING THE CHINESE EARTHQUAKE OF 1905". From the first day we left port, that old tub rolled and lurched with every passing wave causing misery to many. My company was assigned quarters down below on the lowest "deck" of the ship. Between the smell of disinfectant, fuel oil, mold and vomit all over the place, it was awfully hard to keep one's balance let alone one's last meal. We had to take turns with other companies to go up on deck for a breath of fresh air at least one a day. Of course we traveled in a Convoy which took at least ten days to reach our destination, Edinburgh, Scotland.

As I held on to the railing of our Liberty Ship I began to realize how much better off we were in the old tub that sank so deep in the water due to all the weight of men and equipment. Now, on this Liberty Ship which was much smaller, it felt like sitting on a cork in the ocean because the boat was completely empty. I guess they thought they were doing us a favor by putting us on the next ship available to make the trip back to the States – regardless of whether there was any cargo ready to go back too. With just a comparatively few men on board, even the ship's crew had trouble with sea sickness and balance. Twenty foot waves tossed our little "cork" mercilessly about the churning Atlantic as we sailed toward home. Whatever weight we had put on at the hands of the G.I. cooks after being liberated was now being unceremoniously tossed overboard. As land was sighted and the ship pulled into Boston Harbor, we all spruced ourselves up expecting to hear bands playing and people cheering for the return of the conquering heroes.

No such luck! As we pulled into a dock we saw that it was completely empty except for a few Stevedores pushing their hand trucks around. A few girls were seen sitting behind windows doing their office work with an occasional glance in our direction. So, the movies and newsreels were all wrong. No heroes welcome for homecoming troops. Just propaganda. Nobody really cared about who we were or what we had gone through. Talk about being deflated and disillusioned!

As we slowly walked down the gangplank with our meager belongings, several buses pulled up on the wharf. From one emerged a small Army Band of about six or seven men who quickly assembled and started playing. Then a group of Red Cross Ladies appeared who set up a table and began serving coffee and donuts.

That was it! No speeches, no flowers, no heroes welcome – just coffee and donuts, a little Stars and Stripes forever and "get in the buses'. Off to Fort Devens and then on a train to Fort Dix in New Jersey.

Chapter 13

THE ULTIMATE SURPRISE
❧

One of the first things I did when I received my initial Red Cross Parcel at Freising was to write home using the special Red Cross stationary. Thereafter I wrote at least twice a week, telling my folks about my experiences and encouraging them that all was well, I was in one piece and hoped everyone was well at home. Little did I know that those letters I wrote were not getting through. Somehow the letters were lost in transmission. Only a few were delivered to my home weeks after I was already there myself. That was to prove very sad and trying for my family. The uncertainty about my whereabouts or condition ever since they got the first telegram just lingered on. A few days after I was shot my parents received the usual telegram from the War Department – "WE ARE SORRY TO INFORM YOU THAT YOUR SON VAHAN HOVHANNISSIAN HAS BEEN REPORTED MISSING IN ACTION". That was it! No further communication. Not even when we had been liberated had anyone taken the trouble to inform my family that "YOUR SON VAHAN IS NO LONGER MISSING IN ACTION. HE HAS BEEN FOUND ALIVE AND DOING WELL". What a comforting thing that would have been. But alas, such a message was never sent.

The devastation that followed receipt of the "Missing-in-Action" wire was impossible to describe. I found out later that my sister, Lydia, and my older brother, Sudy took it the hardest. My mother and grandmother found courage and strength in their faith. Hadn't they seen worse times? Hadn't they been saved by their unswerving belief the "The Lord is my Shepherd..." Still the gloom that descended on that household was unmistakable. Waiting and wondering for over four months with nary a word as to my fate. The longer the elapsed time without word, the less hope that any good news would ever come.

My sister, with whom I was very close, went to our church more often in those days. She spent more time in prayer and in church activities. She enlisted all those that know me plus many that didn't in prayer vigils. Reverend Houghton was especially diligent in holding prayer meetings for my safety and the safety of all other servicemen from our congregation. He often visited my family to give words of encouragement and to pray with them at the house. Little did they know that their prayers were not in vain. Perhaps it was the intercession of those prayers from across the ocean that led the "Hand of God" to watch over me in so many ways in so many instances. Maybe it wasn't my prayers at all but the congregate voices of many that caught God's ear and led His Hand to me. Or maybe it was a combination of both. In any case, I will forever be thankful to my Lord and Savior for the things he has done for me and for my family before, during and after the tribulations brought on by war.

We were on a troop train going to Fort Dix when I found the train making a stop at the Pennsylvania Station in New York City. As we were sitting there by the platform, the thought struck me to run to the nearest phone and call my folks. The nearest phone was at the head of a staircase, so I positioned one of my buddies at the bottom of the stairs with instructions to signal me when the train was ready to pull out. I then hobbled up to the phone at the top and made my call.

"Hello" my sister answered.

"Hello yourself" I flippantly said, "How is everybody?"

Dead silence.

"Who is this?" came a tentative query.

"It's me. The wandering minstrel. It's me. I'm calling from New York City".

"Oh my God! Mother! It's …its Vahan…I…I…think".

Screams and wails of disbelief and unimaginable happiness broke out over the phone. Incoherent phrases, jumbled voices, tears of joy and non-belief clouded every word.

"You're alive" my mother sobbed, "Johnikus (dear one) you're alive!".

"Yes", I replied, "of course I'm alive" (I had no idea then that they hadn't heard about me) "But we thought" her voice trailed off and I sensed she couldn't speak anymore.

Just then my buddy bounded up the stairs and rapped on the glass door of my phone booth, "the train is leaving!"

"Gotta go now Mom, my train is leaving. Call you later. I love you. Goodbye.

As I hurriedly hung up the phone and hobbled, skipped and bounced down the stairs just as the last car of the train was slowly passing by. My buddy jumped on and held his hand out to me as I shuffled along to keep up with the train. He reached out and grabbed my hand, and, with a big jerk, pulled me aboard just as the train picked up speed.

"We made it" I gasped "Thanks for the helping hand!"

It was a little while later, as I reflected on that phone call, that it came to me – my family didn't even know I was alive! All those months that I had been writing and still, somehow, they didn't know that I was alive. Oh, my God, and I was so flippant with my sister, Lydia. God please forgive me – but how was I to know?

As soon as we were settled in a barracks at Fort Dix I went to the Orderly Room where we were allowed to make one phone call anywhere in the country. This time my mother picked up the phone to which she had been glued ever since my call from Pennsylvania Station.

"Yes, I'm O.K. I was wounded but that's O.K. now. I was a prisoner of war but that's over with. I got back to the States two days ago and now they're getting ready to send me home for 30 days. Be at the Mt. Vernon station Thursday about 3:30. I love you and everyone else. Don't make a fuss. I just want to come home. I miss you all very much".

My father got on the phone for a brief conversation then my grandmother and younger brother, who was born retarded. All said hello and goodbye. My sister was not home and my older brother was still in the service at Joplin, Missouri. By some strange coincidence, my brother's duties at his camp was to guard German Prisoners of War!

The scene at the railroad station was like an instant repeat of my going away. My father, mother, grandmother, sister and brother and my best friend George (who had been 4-F because of his eyes) were all there. Only the girl I left behind wasn't there. That romance had ended with a "Dear John" letter two years earlier. The tears flowed like the Jamestown flood. My nice new uniform with all my medals on display was soon creased and wet from all the hugging and slobbering. Only my walk with a cane gave away the secret of my wounds and feebleness of unrestored muscles.

The partying seemed to go on forever. There was the usual "Welcome Home" banner strung across our living room. Relatives, friends and neighbors streamed in and out with congratulations, greetings, hugs and kisses just like I expected to see in some Bill Holden war movie. And through it all I never saw my mother looking more beautiful. Her smile radiated to every corner of the house. She was so happy that those months of stored up anxiety were now released in a burst of Angelic goodness and love that touched everyone around.

"I told you God would watch over you" she constantly repeated to me and to anyone else that would listen.

That smile alone was worth every bit of suffering, every bit of hardships endured over the last three and a half years. Only an Angel of God could be endowed with such a kind, magnetic, captivating smile that spoke a thousand words without the slightest sound.

That Sunday we all went to church. Reverend Houghton had obviously made preparation because I soon found out that I was the subject of his sermon. Reverend Houghton preached about the Hand of God and how it manifested itself in His Grace. He went on to expound on how God can put his Hand into any situation just by His Grace or in answer to a prayer. After explaining how I had been literally lost and now found (like the words in the hymn Amazing Grace) he asked if I would come forward to say a few words. Being caught off guard, I really stumbled and mumbled before finding the right words. I told the congregation very briefly of my recent hardships and how my prayers had sustained me. I reminded them of the 23rd Psalm which I recited by heart through a landslide of tears and hesitations (mine). And I thanked them all for their prayers of support that surely had been heard. I closed my comments with my living testimony that I have seen the Hand of God; I have held hands with the Hand of God for which I will always be thankful.

Reverend Houghton could find no words to follow my comments even though he was usually quite eloquent. With a choked voice he asked for a moment of silent prayer for those boys that were still unaccounted for or that were never coming home. He then praised God for my safe return and prayed that the Hand of God be there to protect our servicemen wherever they may be. And he reminded everyone that the Hand of God is always there for each one of us – all we have to do is have faith and to reach for it!

THE HAND OF GOD

PART II

The Tamiment Summer Playhouse located in Bushkill, PA, was a prominent incubator of theatrical talents including writers, actors, singers, dancers and comedians who later emerged on the Broadway stage, television, movies and the famous "Borscht Belt". The playhouse spewed such talents as Danny Kaye, Carol Burnett, Woody Allen, Max Liebman, Sid Caesar, Imogene Coca, Shirley Jones, Neil Simon, Dick Shawn and Barbara Cook to mention just a few.

The Theater was part of Camp Tamiment established in 1921 atop a picturesque hilltop complete with a small lake, swimming facilities and a 18 hole golf course. In the early 1930's, the playhouse undertook production of professional, original revues, which eventually became the normal bill-of-fare every weekend. This ambitious program demanded a totally original show every weekend for the entire summer. The format was continued by Max Liebman, one of Tamiment's theatrical directors, who left the camp with two discoveries - Sid Caesar and Imogene Coca. The hit television show that resulted from that union was called "Your Show of Shows" which ran successfully for many seasons.

The Playhouse continued operating until it closed in 1960 – a great loss to aspiring show-biz talents.

After the war, I studied music composition and arranging. One of my teachers ended up asking me if I would like to become a partner in his music school. Never being one to turn down a challenge, my flattered ego encouraged me to accept the offer. The school was called "The Mount Vernon Institute of Cultural Arts". My partners name was George Fragos who wrote a popular song of the day, "I Hear a Rhapsody". After a successful year of teaching, I decided that I would be foolish not to complete my college educa-tion especially since the government would pay for it under the G.I. Bill. I thereupon gave up my partnership after I received acceptance from the college of my choice – Cornell University in Ithaca, New York.

I had two roommates at Cornell, Howard Hochman, who went on to be a very successful veterinarian (we shall hear more about him later), and Ben Josephsen, Jr., whose father was the Director of Camp Tamiment. Taking advantage of this connection, I secured an audition with the playhouse director, Moe Hack. My friend Howard Hochman went with me to the audition and he secured a job as a stage hand. I was hired as a writer/rehearsal pianist. This happened right after my college graduation in June, 1951.

The first week of rehearsals went rather well as we were preparing for our up-coming performance on Saturday night. Late Saturday afternoon, the Director, Moe Hack, announced that one of the spotlight operators had to go to the city and would not be back in time for the performance. My friend Howard was the other spotlight operator for the show. He approached me and said, "since you have nothing to do during the show why not fill in for the missing operator". Not ever having done it before, but in the old spirit of show-biz, I agreed to do it.

Getting to the spotlight loft one had to climb a crude ladder made up of 2 foot boards, nailed onto a support column of the balcony. There was no light switch at the base of the ladder so Howard suggested that I follow him to the loft. He said, 'when we get to the top, there is a cross beam. You stay at the beam while I go ahead to the loft and turn on the light." I followed instructions to wait at the beam with one exception. I decided to step over it and then wait for the light to come on. Little did I know that the cat-walk over the ceiling joists took a sharp left turn on the other side of the beam. It was pitch black but I felt the beam before me and proceeded to step over it. That was a big mistake! As I stepped over the beam I missed the turn of the cat-walk and stepped between the ceiling joists. The flimsy ceiling gave way and down I went approximately 30 feet landing on a row of seats near the front of the auditorium. Now these were very sturdy seats with a cast iron railing that went along the top of the seats connecting the row of seats together.

I don't remember the impact but I do remember regaining consciousness and hearing someone telling me not to move, help is on the way. Eye witnesses later told me that I was a sorry sight laying in a pool of blood and occasionally moaning in pain. They also told me that as soon as I was on my way to the hospital the whole mess was cleared up in time for the show to go on! Again I passed out only to awaken on the floor of a station wagon and hearing a reassuring voice saying. "We're on our way to the hospital. We couldn't wait for the ambulance to come as time is of the greatest importance," the nearest hospital was in Stroudsburg approximately fifteen to twenty miles away. Fortunately for me, the head surgeon, a Dr. Michael Jordan, was called by the camp director, Ben Josephsen, Sr. to come in and take complete charge of my case with no exceptions as to care or cost.

Chapter 14

THE HOSPITAL

The next thing I remember was waking up in a hospital bed the next morning with a nurse at my side who had been there most of the night. As I took inventory of my situation I had to laugh at the sight. I looked just like depicted in the comics about the guy who got the short end of an argument ending up in the hospital with casts and bandaged legs and arms dangling in the air with ropes and pulleys hanging from a network of stainless steel. I could not literally laugh or cry for that matter, because my head and part of my face were swathed in bandages. Nevertheless, I prayed and gave thanks to the Lord that I was still alive. Then another thought crept into my prayers, similar to those that passed my lips on that snow covered battlefield just six years before. When I pull through this will I be a cripple for the rest of my life? Will this put an end to my dreams of a career in Show Business? Questions that were soon to be answered.

I opened my eyes to see Doctor Michael Jordan for the first time. "You sure are one lucky fellow" he said as he leaned over the bed. He could have been an Angel dressed in white softly murmuring over my trussed up body. Standing approximately six feet tall with a full head of silver/gray hair, compassionate blue eyes and a ruddy complexion with worry lines etched in it testifying to his roughly 60 years of caring for others.

"Why was I so lucky?" I asked.

"To begin with, you are lucky to be alive! You lost a lot of blood and broke several bones".

"Like?"

"You landed with your face on the metal backs of those seats. One side of your face was pushed in, the bone over your right eye was fractured and a few teeth were broken.

I was able to restore your shattered cheek bone for now but the rest will take time".

"Have you ever restored a cheek like mine?"

"No, my first time."

"Did you feel that someone was guiding your hand during the operation?"

"Why do you ask?"

"I believe that it was the Hand of God guiding you. Just like His hand guided me as I floated through the air and ended up with the minimal injuries that I got".

"You may be right" said Dr. Jordan, "I was even surprised at the outcome. Now, about your left arm up in the air, there is a cast on your fractured wrist and a pin through the nail of your ring finger because you jammed that finger in the fall and we're trying to pull it back out to normal length with a big rubber band attached to that wire on your cast."

It certainly looked like a "Rube Goldberg" affair with a wire hoop attached to the cast extending forward with a large rubber band coming back to pull on the pin through my ring finger.

"Will I be able to play the piano again?" I asked.

"Probably but with limited use of that finger. You also cracked three ribs which is why you have a body bandage on. They will take time to heal. You also smashed in your right hip. That's why we have one weight pulling down on your leg and another pulling sideways. There are no leg bones broken by the impact but your hip socket was severely crushed in. It is really amazing how your thigh bone did not break but was strong enough to push the socket in. This may cause you considerable trouble as you get older."

"And you don't think that the Hand of God was present throughout this whole ordeal?" Then I began relating some of my near-death experiences and how my faith and trust in the Hand of God guarded and protected me during and even after going through whatever hardships and pain that confronted me..

Dr. Jordan's look of amazement was evident in all our future talks on the subject. It finally got to the point where he began to believe the "power of prayer" to such an extent that he passed it on to his future patients. Provided the subject was willing, he instituted a policy of praying with his patient before every major surgical procedure. Perhaps that was the reason for my accident. God always has a plan and purpose, not readily apparent to our part in His Plan, using us to accomplish His purpose.

Perhaps the most convincing story about The Hand of God was my being shot. As he traced the trajectory of the bullet going in one leg, hitting the bone and turning (without breaking it), exiting that leg sideways, entering the other leg sideways and exiting that leg flattened out, all while traveling on a line that should have demolished my private parts! Fortunately, I was lying on my stomach and gravity had a hand in fooling disaster. Nevertheless, it has been a source of wonderment then and down through the years – a hard to believe miracle.

Chapter 15

JANICE BY DAY

The next two months became rather routine what with being bathed, changing bandages, adjusting weights on the stretching ropes, visitors and, of course, bed pans. One bright spot was the staff of very pretty nurses and aides. Of special note were my day-time nurse, Janice, and my night-time nurse, Betty. Janice spent a good deal of extra time in my room asking questions about my work and the Tamiment Playhouse. A shapely brunette in her mid twenties who lived not far from the hospital, Janice was always pert and cheerful when entering my room. In many ways she brought back fond memories of the bubbling nurse, Helga, who always brought sunshine to my room when I was a POW/MIA in a German Hospital during the war.

My folks were notified of the accident (after all operations and examinations were complete). My mother, older brother and sister came the next day with understandable worried looks and frowns on their faces. Only my sister broke out in a giggle commenting on the bazaar comic picture of me with all my bandages, casts, weights and ropes. My mother was put at ease after conferring with Dr. Jordan and the nurses. Of course, she had to bring the required basket of Armenian 'goodies' with the sure knowledge that I must be starving. As a matter of fact, I was getting hungry since my diet so far was liquid. Not-withstanding a few broken teeth in my mouth, Dr. Jordan didn't want chewing motion to disturb the good work he had done restoring my shattered cheek.

Before departing, my family and I prayed together thanking the Lord for looking after me and praying for my continued healing back to health.

Now getting back to Nurse Janice. I really can't describe what a help she was to me. She helped me change positions in the bed, even found a comfortable way to use the bed pan. She got me a sheep's skin semi-sheet to ease the painful bed sores I developed. Perhaps the "touchiest" procedure was giving me a daily sponge bath. When it came time, she would hand me the washcloth to do my "private parts". This of course led to a "show-n-tell" about my bullet wounds. Again, that particular display of incredible proof of the guiding hand of God was the subject and object of much discussion and wonderment. Doctors, interns, nurses and administrators began a stream of curious examinations and observations of a phenomenon never before seen. Now it wasn't very long before Janice assumed the informal duties of 'director' and classroom guide, explaining in medical and lay terms how unique this alignment of bullet wounds as testicles was so incongruous.

Notwithstanding the humorous aspects of my hospital stay, I did find myself growing fonder of her every day, especially after my left arm was relieved of its high perch and relegated to a sling. It was then possible for me to stop wearing hospital gowns and put on my own pajamas. I could only wear the tops because my right leg was still married to the ropes and pulley trying to pull out my hip joint. I only had one pair of pajamas, so, after the third week, Janice offered to take them home at the end of her shift, wash them and return them the next morning. In the meantime, I had to wear a hospital gown overnight. Now this news got around very fast and several of the other nurses said to me, "Janice has never done that before. She must really like you." I assume that it's not in the nurse's handbook to take a patients P.J.s home, launder and iron them, and return them the next day. I could see that I was heading for a potential problem so I turned my attention to nurse Betty.

Chapter 16

BETTY BY NIGHT

B etty, my often night nurse (they kept shifting them around) was also very attractive and efficiently attentive to my needs. Although a little older than the other nurses, (maybe early thirties), Betty carried her shorter, stockier body very well. With natural blond hair and a ruddy complexion, her short, pudgy fingers were a testimony to her manual abilities and diligent work ethics. She would glide from room to room, with a slightly hurried pace, making sure that her charges were comfortable and ready for a good night's sleep. Fortunately, I was in a private room which meant I had Betty all to myself when she swished through the doorway.

On those occasions that I had trouble sleeping, Betty would keep me company after her other patients were comfortably dispatched to "la-la land". We would talk about serious and mundane topics alike. Having a good college education before nursing school, she was quite well informed on a great variety of subjects. However, one night she abruptly changed the subject of our conversation to Janice.

Evidently the word about the pajamas got around to the night shift because Betty point blank asked me "Are you going for Janice? She's a sweet girl and everybody is wishing a man would come into her life. You know, she recently broke up with her fiancée and hasn't had the desire to have another relationship for the last few months." "No" I replied, "I have no intentions of getting serious at this stage of my life. I've got a career to cultivate and a romantic entanglement would only be an obstacle."

"But", she said. "I heard about some lengthy handholding between you two".

"Oh that, someone must have seen us when I was reading her palm"

"You do that?"

"Yes, I do palm reading but it's only for fun and entertainment. According to the Bible, we are not to believe in, or engage in, any type of witchcraft or the occult so don't take anything I say seriously."

"Tell my fortune anyway" as she thrust her hand into my face. Now, I was compelled to relate what I saw in the lines of her delicate little hand and all was not positive. I cut off the reading when I saw a shortened life line telling her I was getting tired. She said she understood and would be back later so I could continue. The 'later' came shortly thereafter since she was so anxious to learn more. I couldn't tell her what I saw but made up a story about her lines being too indistinct for an adequate reading. That seemed to satisfy her for the moment. But then started the stream of nurses who heard about the reading and wanted their own palms read. I must admit I enjoyed the attention and popularity but soon got tired. Realizing that I was drooping, Betty took charge and began screening the prospective 'fortune seekers'.

On many nights our conversation would touch on religion. Betty, a devout Catholic, would ask how I could be so sure of my journey in this life and in the life beyond.

"Look at all the hardships and near-death experiences in your life. Would a caring God put you through all that pain and suffering?"

"It's because he has allowed these things to happen to me" I said, that my faith has grown stronger. When I surrendered my life to Christ, I realized that He was in control and whatever He let happen to me had to have a good reason".

"Is that what they mean when they talk about Being Born Again?

"Exactly", I said, "and it is available to anyone who earnestly asks for it regardless of what denomination you believe in". Betty would ponder over these conversations until one night when she told me that she was ready to find what I had. I asked her to kneel by my bed and repeat the words I would say asking Jesus into her heart as Lord and Master. She cried. I cried. And I said, "You are now my sister in Christ. Praise the Lord."

Betty seemed to change after that night. She seemed less concerned about her love life, her Mother's illness and life in general. I thanked God that perhaps I played a small part in Betty's happiness and future.

Meanwhile, although Janice hadn't told anyone about my reading her palm, the news spread from the night shift to the day shift and the parade started right after breakfast.

So now I had audience coming to see my wounds and another parade of 'fortune' seekers. All in all, a very interesting daily routine developing that made my lengthy stay quite bearable.

Chapter 17

WHO WOULD HAVE THOUGHT

It was almost three months now and I knew I would be discharged any day. One of my biggest concerns was how to gracefully say 'goodbye' without seeming callous and ungrateful. The problem was quickly solved when, one day, Dr. Jordan announced I could go home. Fortunately, it was day time so I didn't have to worry about Betty. And Janice – it was her normal day off so she would see me gone the next day. That morning they took me downtown to a very good Dentist who fixed my broken teeth and filled the gaps with solid gold fillings! My first luxurious fillings and they are still in my mouth as good as the day they were put in.

I was released from the hospital on crutches with strict instructions to go slow. My friend Howard came to pick me up in my car and drove me back to camp. The theatrical crew was quite happy to see me even though many of them had visited me in the hospital. I saw the last two shows of the season and it became apparent that they didn't miss my services.

Now one of the girls on the production staff (I will not mention her name) came to visit me at the hospital more than anyone else. She 'mothered' me about the camp making sure that I maneuvered around on my crutches without incident. One night, after watching the last show together, she invited me to her cabin. Not knowing what to expect, I neverthe-less hobbled along wondering how could I possibly manage if the occasion should arise. Well, the occasion did arise as soon as she closed and locked the cabin door. Without even asking me if I was willing or able, she proceeded to undress. I said, "I don't know if I can do this in my present condition." She murmured back, "Oh, you would be surprised at what you can do with a little will power and imagination." She thereupon took my crutches away, sat me on the edge of the bed and cooed "now just relax and follow my lead." No one was more willing to follow instructions at that point so I proceeded to perform! Meanwhile, I couldn't help wondering if anyone else had ever had this delightful experience while on crutches. No matter, with some painstaking movements that were completely masked by intense pleasure, I performed my part with ultimate satisfaction. As I lay there in the ecstasy of the moment, I wondered did I commit myself to this woman. I know the attraction was strictly physical and I definitely didn't want a relationship that would hinder my career. So I played it cool.

As everyone in the cast was leaving the next day, she queried me about seeing each other in the city. I must have mumbled some assent because we parted like long-lost lovers. It was not hard to avoid seeing her soon because I stayed on at the camp a few more weeks as a guest of the Josephsens. Many messages awaited my return home and I politely returned her calls. However, I had no plans to travel to the city even though I had now graduated to walking with a cane. The final severance of our relationship came when I decided to return to Cornell in order to finish production of a show I had started before graduation. That accomplished with a successful performance in the spring of 1952, I turned my attention to opening an office in 'Tin-Pan-Alley' with another very talented buddy from Cornell, who went on to the Julliard School of Music before we teamed up.

Like pieces of a jig-saw puzzle, my life was falling into place just as I and the Master of my life had planned. All my injuries were clearing up and healing, and, my music career was rapidly gaining momentum. I thank God every day for His faithful attention to my prayers and His skillful guidance that enabled me to overcome all my injuries and regain all my mental and physical abilities. Even my experience with that un-named girl at the camp convinced me that, once again, someone was watching over me.

The Hand of God, ever loving and ever faithful, is available to any believer who wants it, who needs it and sincerely asks for it. Remember the door to your heart only has a knob on the inside. You must willingly open it to invite Jesus in and surrender your life to His guidance. Try it – it has, and is still, working for me!

BIOGRAPHY

VAHAN HOVEY

V ahan Hovey came, with his parents, to this country, in 1928 at the age of three from his mother country, Armenia.

His creative talents soon became apparent especially his ear for music which enabled him to perform his first concert while still in kindergarten at the age of five. After graduating from High School, Vahan volunteered for the army in 1942 and served in Europe in the 12th armored division. He was shot in combat, taken prisoner by the Germans and was a POW/MIA until the war's end in 1945. After completing his college education at Cornell University, he immediately opened an office in the heart of the music business known as Tin Pan Alley. There he wrote music for acts as well as various songs that were published and recorded. His associations included the Benny Goodman Family; Connie Francis; the Andrew Sisters; Roy Rogers; the Bon Bons and many more. He also collaborated with Mitch Miller in song writing including a number recorded by Rosemary Clooney.

Vahan is still actively writing music having had a recent album of kiddie songs recorded by Dom DeLuise called "Gimme A Smile". He has also written a biblically based musical that he hopes to have produced in the near future.

Printed in the United States
150695LV00002B/2/P